Soul food

for the

Entrepreneur

Nataleh Howard

Table of Contents

Jeremiah 29:11 NIV

"For I know the plans I have for you", declares the Lord, "plans to prosper you and not to harm you, plans to give you hope and a future".

Preface

Are you ready to grow in your business and in the promises of God?

This devotional was written for the entrepreneur who is ready to take a leap of faith and incorporate God into every part of their business. Through this devotional you will learn how to apply biblical principles to your business to maximize your income and success. Be Spirit-Led as you read this devotional and allow for the Holy Spirit to really work in your life and business. Open your heart and mind to receive what God has for you. Lastly, be prepared for God to move in a mighty way not only in your business, but in your everyday life.

Be blessed,

Nataleh

Section 1: Before the Business

Starting a business of your own is a beautiful thing. It allows you freedom in many areas of your life. You have the ability to gain freedom in your day-to-day schedule, and in your finances. But it's important that before we spend time focusing on your business, we spend some time making sure you are prepared for what you are getting ready to build.

A house built on a rocky foundation is not guaranteed to withstand a storm of any kind. The home's foundation must be strong; the same goes for your business!

You have what it takes to be successful, but true success will come when you have taken the time to plant your business on a solid foundation.

So, before we get into business building strategies, take the next 5 days to strengthen your core, cleanse your mind, and get ready to receive all that God is getting ready to do in and through what you build.

Throughout the duration of this devotional, remain open to what God wants to speak to you and do in your life!

This book will equip you with scriptures to back up each step in this process, while also providing prayers to help you through each phase.

Meditate on the scriptures, pray the prayers, and most importantly journal your thoughts at the end of each day's devotion. The journaling aspect of this devotional is meant for you to have an intimate time with God. So, don't skip any steps and watch what God does in your life and business!

Follow along each day, and you will start to see amazing changes in your life, and your finances!

Day 1: Way too Big Dreams!

"For My thoughts are not your thoughts, nor are your ways My ways," declares the Lord. "For as the heavens are higher than the earth, so are My ways higher than your ways and My thoughts than your thoughts." Isaiah 55: 8-9 NASB

Before starting your business, you must submit your thoughts, ideas, and dreams to God. Your thoughts and doubts could have you believe that you are not equipped to start a business. Yes, starting a business from scratch can appear overwhelming, but just like the scripture for today states, God's ways are higher than your ways. His thoughts are higher than your thoughts.

Don't think it's strange that you have these huge desires that seem way too big for your life. God can see your now, your past, and your future. No matter what you believe about yourself, God created you for a purpose. You may see yourself as insignificant, but God sees you as the perfect person for the job. You may think you are not qualified, but to God you have exactly what it takes.

We can't see what God sees. We can't understand how he understands. His thoughts are higher. Synonyms for higher are giant, excessive, outrageous, big, and costly. To our human minds, God's thoughts seem outrageous.

So, if you've questioned your dreams; if you thought your ideas were way too big for you, just know you're in the right place. Your "too big" dreams line up exactly with who God is. They're meant to be huge. They're meant to be bigger than what you yourself can do. This is why we have God. This is why we need God. Nothing is impossible for him. Declare to yourself: "Nothing is impossible to God. With God, I will achieve my dreams". Now believe it as if it's already done.

Prayer: Lord I submit every idea and dream that I have to you now! I pray that whatever idea or dream I have that does not line up with your will for my life, take it away now in Jesus Name. Lord, make your desires, my desires! Show me the thoughts that you have for my life. Increase my faith. Help me to believe that no matter how big your plans are for my life; they will come to pass. I recognize that you are almighty. You are all knowing. You are all powerful. You created the heavens and the earth. You created me. Nothing is impossible for you. With you God, I will achieve all my dreams. I will be successful. I pray that throughout this entire process, you remain by my side. In Jesus Name. Amen.

Write to God

List out your desires and dreams. No matter how big or small, write down what is on your heart. What have you dreamed of doing, but you've been too afraid to give it your all? Write a letter to God now concerning this area of your life.

Dear God,
I dream of sharing my story to millions, A smart black girl who know what it feels like to see 1 footprint in life. My drive and love for people headlining my success story. Women's empowerment to restore the Black woman, Through Book and action. My desire is to help those who I can't imagine paying back. 6 figure minimum Everything I was told I couldn't, ~

I Did!

a mom that
leah is proud of
I will give her
and her kids a
foundation only
imagineable. The
house that is
built from hand

My goal is to find time to
workout and Lose weight
naturally. Take the trading
world by storm! A woman
who trades,

Day 2: Pray Right to Heaven!

"If My people, who are called by My Name, humble themselves, pray and seek (crave, require as a necessity) My face and turn from their wicked ways, then I will hear [them] from heaven... Now My eyes will be open and My ears attentive to prayer offered in this place." 2 Chronicles 7: 13-15 AMP

Wow. 2 Chronicles 7 says that God will hear you from heaven. Not only that, but he will be attentive to your payers. Attentive means to pay close attention to. It also means to attend to the comfort or wishes of others. God will attend to your comfort and wishes! How amazing is that. Other words for attentive are mindful, wide awake, and on the lookout. Can you imagine God being wide awake towards your request? God will be on the lookout for your prayers!

How many times have you prayed the same prayer over and over, and felt like you were speaking to a brick wall? Have you ever felt unheard? God loves you and he even wants to pay close attention to you and your business. But first, you must follow his instructions. All God wants is your attention. He wants you to pray to him, and to seek him out. I love how the amplified version explains what seek means. To seek is to crave; to require God as a necessity.

Can you admit that you need God? Can you tell God that you want him in your life? James 4:8 reads "Draw near to God and he will draw near to you". I know sometimes it can feel like God isn't near, or maybe he's near you, but He is choosing not to hear your prayer. Have you ever felt like God is forgetting you? Well he hasn't. But we must do our part.

Not only do we have to commit to pray and seek God, but we must also turn from our wicked ways. This commitment is crucial for having God hear us. God doesn't hate you; he hates sin.

It's time to make a decision. Do you want to please yourself and continue living your own life, in your own way? Or, do you want to please God? Are you ready for God to hear your prayers? Do you want God to show up in your personal life and in your business? If you answered yes, then you are ready to complete each prerequisite listed in 2 Chronicles 7: 13-15.

1.Humble yourself: In this instance, to humble oneself means to admit that you need God. To even admit that you've done things your own way, and now you are ready to do it God's way.

2.Pray: make it a point to pray to God often. If you are unsure where to start, start by reading the prayer of the day every single day.

3.Seek God's face: To seek is to crave, and to require God as a necessity. How bad do you want God in your life? How much do you need him? Declare today that you want God to show up every day in your life and that you need him! Include God in everything you do!

4.Turn from your wicked ways: This simply means to turn away from all sin. Repent. To leave the world's way of doing things behind and commit to living life God's way.

Prayer: God today I give everything to you. I give my life to you. I give my heart to you. I am committed to living a life that is pleasing to you. I pray that you forgive me for all of my sins that I have committed against you whether I knowingly, or unknowingly committed the sin. Help me to turn from everything that is not pleasing to you, and to seek you more. Give me the desire to seek you! Help me pray to you every day. I ask that as I seek you every day, that you are right there with me. As I pray, God let your ears be attentive to me. Let your eyes be on me and my business now. I humble myself before you, and I admit that I need you. I cannot do this without you. I don't want to do this without you. I thank you now for hearing me. I thank you now for blessing me. In Jesus Name, Amen!

Write to God

How do you plan to seek God more? What can you commit to turn from that is not pleasing to God? Ask God for forgiveness. As soon as you've asked for forgiveness, you are forgiven. Now write out the prayers to God that you've maybe prayed in the past, but they've been left unanswered. God hears you now. Write a letter to Him.

I will talk to God through prayer in the Am when I first wake up 3 at night and also before each financial decision through the day. I pray for him to release only thing not of his image

Day 3: God's Promises to You

"And now that you belong to Christ, you are the true children (seed) of Abraham. You are his heirs, and God's promises to Abraham belongs to you" Galatians 3:29 NLT

"God heard their groaning, and he remembered his covenant promise to Abraham, Isaac, and Jacob. He looked down on the people of Israel and knew it was time to act" Exodus 2:25 NLT

- Here this also meant he acknowledged his obligation to help them.

"You will show us your faithfulness and unfailing love as you promised to our ancestors Abraham and Jacob long ago" Micah 7:20 NLT

In the book of Genesis there was a man named Abraham who God promised to bless. He promised to bless him to be father of many nations. He also promised to bless the land of his family. The promise was not only for Abraham but also for his son Isaac and all of his descendants.

Now this blessing was such a huge deal (and still is!) because at the time Abraham and his wife Sarah were old in age. They far exceeded childbearing age. They hadn't bore any children together at this time, but God made them a promise! God's promise did not happen right away! As Abraham and Sarah waited to bear a child, they continued to get older in age. But nonetheless, Abraham kept his faith! And as he kept his faith, God kept his promise!

Now why is this important? I want you to really understand what the scriptures above are showing us. The promises that God gave to Abraham to bless his family and their land did not just stop with Abraham and his son Isaac. God has continually honored his FULL promise over many years; that he will bless every descendant of Abraham.

As you are starting your business, it is important for you to understand how this applies to your life. As you live in Christ, the promise of Abraham applies to you as well. God promises to bless you and everything you own. That includes your home, your family, and your business.

Exodus 2:25 reads "God heard their groaning, and he remembered his covenant promise to Abraham, Isaac, and Jacob. He looked down on the people of Israel and knew it was time to act". On day 2 we learned how to have our prayers reach heaven, and now you understand that because of whose you are (Jesus Christ), your prayers will not only be heard but they will be answered. God keeps his promises! Because of the promise he made, he will act on your behalf!

As we go into building our business God's way understand that God promises to bless it! At any point in this process you have the right to remind God of the covenant promise he made to Abraham, and how that promise applies to you. Apply this principle to your business, to your home, to your family, and to every aspect of your personal life! You are blessed.

Prayer: God, I thank you for choosing to bless me. Thank you for the inheritance that is passed down to me because of the promise you gave to Abraham. Just as you blessed Abraham, Lord I pray that you bless me. Bless my family, bless my home, and Lord bless my business in Jesus name. Thank you for hearing my prayer. In Jesus Name, Amen.

Write to God

Today simply write to God and express to him every area of your life where you need a blessing. Thank God for what he has already done and what he will do soon.

_____

_____

_____

_____

_____

_____

_____

_____

_____

_____

_____

_____

_____

_____

Day 4: How's Your Foundation?

"Therefore, everyone who hears these words of Mine and acts on them, may be compared to a wise man who built his house on the rock. And the rain fell, and the floods came, and the winds blew and slammed against that house; and yet it did not fall, for it had been founded on the rock. Everyone who hears these words of Mine and does not act on them, will be like a foolish man who built his house on the sand. The rain fell, and the floods came, and the winds blew and slammed against that house; and it fell - and great was its fall"
Matthew 7: 24-27 NASB

What is your business built on? Is it being built on your own knowledge? Is it being built on the knowledge of a trusted mentor? Or is it being built on the word of God? The entire purpose of this devotional is to allow for you to have the opportunity to understand what God says about you, your business, and your legacy.

As we get closer to the building stage for your business, continue to seek God. Before wondering what anyone else says, ask what God said! I'm not saying it's wrong to learn from other people! Learning from others and their experiences can be wise. But before you go out and gain wisdom from other people, be sure that your business is built on a solid foundation. That solid foundation is the word of God.

As we read from the scripture today, a foolish man's house cannot withstand any trials or storms. Your business's foundation must be solid. I've made a point to include scriptures every day so that you are reading the word of God as you plan your business. Continue doing the groundwork to ensure that your business can withstand any turmoil, rain, or obstacles that may come along your journey.

This can mean taking the scripture of the day and then taking some time to read the entire chapter to study more of God's word. This can also look like you taking the prayers of the day and saying them over yourself repeatedly throughout the day.

Do the work now, so God's hand can stay over your business as you grow!

Prayer: God plant my business on a firm foundation! I pray that as I build my business, I have a solid foundation under me so I can withstand any storm. I pray your hedge of protection guards my business, my mind, and my finances as I give my business ideas over to you today. Bless me now as I seek you. In Jesus Name, Amen!

Write to God

What can you commit to do so that your business is put on a solid foundation? Write it out and after you journal, do those things! Seek God.

_____

_____

_____

_____

_____

_____

_____

_____

_____

_____

_____

_____

_____

_____

_____

Day 5: The Secret to Your Business Success

"But the Helper (Comforter, Advocate, Intercessor-Counselor, Strengthener, Standby), the Holy Spirit, whom the Father will send in My name [in My place, to represent Me and act on My behalf], he will teach you all things. And He will help you remember everything that I have told you" John 14:26 AMP

"That is what the Scriptures mean when they say, "No eye has seen, no ear has heard, and no mind has imagined what God has prepared for those who love him." But it was to us that God revealed these things by his Spirit. For his Spirit searches out everything and show us God's deep secrets." 1 Corinthians 2:9-10 NLT

1 Corinthians 2 explains how there are secret things that only God knows. We haven't heard, seen, or even THOUGHT about the amazing and great things that God wants to do in us and through our lives. God has so many plans for our lives, and unless we know how to access the secrets of God, we could be stuck feeling like we want to do more but have no idea what that more is! Have you ever experienced that feeling? You know there's more to your life; more to your family's life… but you have no idea how to access it. If so, you're missing one crucial person, the Holy Spirit. Let's dive deeper into the word.

Verse 11 of this passage goes on to say, No one can know a person's thoughts except that person's own spirit, and no one can know God's thoughts except God's own spirit. Verse 12 And we have received God's spirit (not the world's spirit), so we can know the wonderful things God has freely given us. We as believers have direct access to the thoughts and deep secrets of God. But we don't just know them because we know and love God. We must understand how this works… to gain access to the intimate thoughts of God, we must ask his Holy Spirit to reveal them to us.

The Holy Spirit is a gift given to us when Jesus left the earth. Through God's spirit we can receive insight in every area of our lives. As we gear up to build and grow our business, the help of the Holy Spirit will be mandatory to have a God-blessed business.

With the Holy Spirit, nothing is impossible for us. Nothing will ever be too difficult. Nothing will be too hard to obtain or understand. We now have a secret weapon to supernatural success. The Holy Spirit. Invite Him into your life today. Invite Him into your business. Invite Him into your family.

Prayer: God I thank you for gifting me with your Holy Spirit. I am so thankful for having direct access to you through your Holy Spirit. I invite your Holy Spirit into my life today. I invite your Spirit into my business, and every area of my life right now in Jesus Name. I pray that your Holy Spirit reveals to me the ideas and plans that you have for my life. Lord, begin to give me supernatural thoughts and ideas that are coming directly from you. Show me what you want me to achieve today! Show me what you want me to work on today. Give me specific instructions and directions from your Holy Spirit right now. I pray that you bless my ears (touch your ears) so that I can hear you clearly. I pray that you bless my mind (touch your head) so that I can clearly think the thoughts you have for me. I pray that you bless my eyes (touch your eyes) so that I can see the path you've clearly paved for me. Lead me and guide me Holy Spirit. In Jesus Name, Amen.

Write to God

Write a letter to God and the Holy Spirit. After praying, continue to talk to the Holy Spirit and let him know in what area you invite him in today. Whether it's your heart, your job, your relationship, wherever you need help, invite the Holy Spirit in. He's a present help. But he's also a perfect gentleman and will only come where you allow. Write to Him.

Section 2: Building the Business

Now that we've set the foundation, it's time to build the business.

Although we will focus on building the business in this section, building doesn't have to mean that you are new.

Whether you are brand new to business, or you're someone who has a business and are ready to do it God's way, this section will aid you in ensuring you don't lose faith or hope in this phase of your business.

Day 6: What Business to Start?

"I knew you before I formed you in your mother's womb. Before you were born, I set you apart and appointed you as my prophet to the nations." Jeremiah 1:5 NLT

Are you someone who's questioned the type of business you want to start? Maybe you know you want to become an entrepreneur, but you are unsure what business to start with? Although God was talking specifically to the Prophet Jeremiah in today's scripture, the same goes for you. God knew who you were before you were born, even before you were formed in your mother's womb.

You see, everything about who you are and where you came from was strategically planned by God. He created you for a purpose, just how he created Jeremiah to be a prophet to the nations. Understand that God created you with a specific purpose in mind. He put you on this earth to solve a specific problem. It's time to ask the Holy Spirit exactly what problem you are meant to solve. Ask Him what is your purpose.

I once had no idea what my purpose was. As I was getting ready to graduate college, I finally sought out God and asked him to reveal my purpose to me. I was desperate. I fasted for 3 days and prayed day and night. Finally, I had a memory; a very faint one. I remembered that when I was a little girl, I wanted to be a teacher. I had to be in maybe 1st grade or maybe even younger, and I dressed up as a teacher for career day. From a young age I had such a strong desire to teach. I knew God was showing me the plan he had for me.

So, I became a teacher in the classroom, and now I teach entrepreneurship. I turned my purpose into a career and a business. Although your purpose can directly tie to your business, it doesn't have to! Yes, I teach business now, but I started off by opening an online clothing store simply because I loved fashion and styling. Loving fashion may not be a specific purpose of mine, but I enjoyed it and felt peace about pursuing it, so I went with it.

About 3 months into running my clothing business, God naturally positioned me on YouTube to start teaching aspiring entrepreneurs how to open their own clothing store. I started off just running a clothing business, but in the end God's purpose for my life came back to the surface. In every area of my business, I teach.

So simply put, decide on a business.

You can consider what you're gifted in, or what you are purposed to do, but have peace in knowing that whatever God has planned for your life, it will happen. In the end, God has the ultimate power. So, choose a business, and let's get started!

Prayer: Lord, I thank you for creating me for a purpose. I thank you for having your hand over my life. I pray that you give me peace on a business decision. Lord, whatever business I decide to start, I pray now that you use it for your good. Lead me back to your ultimate purpose for my life. Show me your purpose for my life. Show me your plans for my life. Reveal the secret things of you through your Holy Spirit. Guide me down the right path. If I desire something that you don't want me to do, completely take the desires and the plans away in Jesus Name. I commit my business to you now. In Jesus Name, Amen.

Write to God

As you pray to God, write out your thoughts. What plans do you think God has for your life? What are you naturally good at? What do you get excited to do? What do you feel your ultimate purpose is? If you don't know, don't force it. Pray to God to reveal it over time, and, in the meantime, write down what you are good at and what you enjoy doing. Write out your ideal business plans, no matter how big or small they may be. God is in control. Anything is possible!

_____

_____

_____

_____

_____

_____

_____

_____

_____

_____

Day 7: You Are Creative

Then God said, "Let Us (Father, Son, Holy Spirit) make man in Our image, according to Our likeness [not physical, but a spiritual personality and moral likeness] ..." Genesis 1:26 AMP

We were created in the exact image of God. God wanted his people to be made just like him. Not physically, but in every other attribute. The main characteristic of God is his creativity. Have you ever looked at something and just wondered how in the world that could be created? Like a mother's womb. How can a human really grow inside of someone else? How did the sky turn out to be blue? You see, God has always been creative. He created the heavens and the earth. He created you and me.

If our Father is creative, and we were made in his Image, we too are creative! We also have the ability to create something out of nothing. Just how God used his words to create life, we too can use our words to create (but we will learn more about the power of our words later!).

No matter how impossible your business plans and ideas may seem, realize you are creative just like your Father in heaven. Your business is not too big for you to handle. You serve a big God; whose thoughts are greater than yours. You have a Helper who knows the thoughts and plans of God. You are God's beloved child, so the promises of God are yours! Believe that your business ideas are possible, no matter how big they may seem.

Prayer: Father I thank you for creating me in your image. Thank you for being a creator, and in turn making me creative. I declare that my business dreams are not too big for you to handle. I pray that you are by my side throughout every step in this business process so that I may accomplish every dream and idea that you've given to me. I allow your Holy Spirit into my business today. In Jesus Name, Amen!

Write to God

Start to write out the details to how your business or business growth will get created. Remember you are creative. You can get this done!

_____

_____

_____

_____

_____

_____

_____

_____

_____

_____

_____

_____

_____

_____

_____

_____

Day 8: Wisdom from God

If any of you lack wisdom, you should ask God, who gives
generously to all without finding fault, and it will be given to you.
James 1:5 NIV

Today you have the power and ability to ask God for wisdom. No matter what, he gives wisdom generously! Wisdom is defined as the quality of having experience, knowledge, and good judgment.

Wow.

Imagine being new in your perspective industry, but because of God's wisdom you now have the quality of being experienced, having knowledge, and able to make good judgment calls. That is the true benefit of making God your CEO. No matter how new you are, you can be seen as an expert in your field. The wisdom of God far exceeds the knowledge of man.

Are you feeling defeated? Do you feel confusion on the next steps to take in your business? Ask God for Wisdom in every area of your life! Receive the wisdom of God. God's thoughts are higher than men. Even if you know the steps, invite God's wisdom into your business and allow it to take your business to levels you never even dreamed of.

Prayer: Lord thank you for being all knowing. Thank you for knowing the ins and outs of every detail of my life. I pray that you give me supernatural wisdom in the area of my business. Show me ways to grow and expand my business far above what I can even imagine. I pray that you give me supernatural God-given wisdom to understand and know how to grow my finances. I trust that you are showing and telling me now. In Jesus Name, Amen.

Write to God

Push away all distractions and allow your mind to be clear. Once your mind is clear, pray for wisdom again, and write down every thought and idea you have concerning your life, business, and your finances.

_____

_____

_____

_____

_____

_____

_____

_____

_____

_____

_____

_____

_____

Day 9: What is Faith?

But when you ask, you must believe and not doubt, because the one who doubts is like a wave of the sea, blown and tossed by the wind. That person should not expect to receive anything from the Lord. Such a person is double-minded and unstable in all they do. James 1:6-7 NIV

God is very clear on his stance with Faith. We've learned so much about the promises of God, and all that he wants to do for us, but it is impossible to truly receive the things of God unless we believe for what we ask for.

We read the earlier part of this passage yesterday, when we learned about asking for Wisdom. Yes, God wants to bless us with knowledge, and blessings, and many other things, but we must believe in order to receive. The scripture says that the person who doubts should not expect to receive anything from the Lord.

Your business has no place for doubt. Doubt equates to failure. You must believe now that you will be successful. Believe now that God is walking you through each step. Believe now that your business will reach the next level. As you believe, ask God for wisdom to make it happen.

Fix your mind first, and then approach God. Go to God with expectation, and then make your request known. God gives freely to his people, and his people believe that he will do just that.

Prayer: Lord I put my complete faith in you now. I believe everything that you've said to me in your word. I thank you now for blessing me with the gift of Faith. I declare all doubt must leave my mind now. Doubt has no right and no place in my life. I come to you in complete faith. I thank you for the business ideas you are giving to me now. I thank you for the business success you are blessing me with now. Thank you, God, for faith. In Jesus Name, Amen.

Write to God

Write down everything that you are believing God for in FAITH. As you write down each item, push doubt away. You can receive anything! But you must believe God. If you feel doubt, touch your head and declare it to leave your mind immediately and believe that it is gone. Now place your mind on God and know he can do all things, in Jesus Name

_____

_____

_____

_____

_____

_____

_____

_____

_____

_____

_____

_____

_____

Day 10: Your Source

"Remain in me, as I also remain in you. No branch can bear fruit by itself; it must remain in the vine. Neither can you bear fruit unless you remain in me. I am the vine; you are the branches. If you remain in me and I in you, you will bear much fruit; apart from me you can do nothing". John 15: 4-5 NIV

In this passage, fruit means answered prayer, as mentioned in verse 7. While growing your business it is key to keep Jesus at the center of it all. For without Him, your business will bear no fruit. Without Christ, there are no answered prayers. Without God there is no business success. Without the Holy Spirit, your business will have no true wisdom or plan.

God must stay at the center of everything you do. It is important to remember that while you are building. Continue to seek the face of God concerning your business. Continue to turn from your wicked ways. Continue to pray. Don't lose hope.

Building anything from scratch can be an overwhelming task from a human point of view but remember whom you serve. As a child of God, you have to come out on top. It's the promise that God gave Abraham back in the book of Genesis. Don't forget who you are; WHOSE you are!

Prayer: God I thank you that you are in me, as I remain in you. I thank you God for allowing me to bear fruit in everything I do. I pray that my business bears supernatural fruit that will increase the influence, impact, and income that I have. I dedicate my life, and my business to you now. I love you Lord. In Jesus Name, Amen.

Write to God

Today just write to God and admit to him that you need him. Write to him your intimate thoughts.

_____

_____

_____

_____

_____

_____

_____

_____

_____

_____

_____

_____

_____

_____

_____

Day 11: Do it in Jesus' Name

"If you remain in me and my words remain in you, ask whatever you wish, and it will be done for you." John 15:7

"You did not choose me, but I chose you and appointed you so that you might go and bear fruit-fruit that will last-and so that whatever you ask in my name the Father will give you." John 15:16

It's important that you understand the principles of asking and receiving. The person speaking in John 15 is Jesus Christ, the Son of God. Too often we want to focus on the latter part of John 15: 7 "ask whatever you wish, and it will be done", but we cannot read the good without reading Jesus's specific instructions.

We must remain in Christ. God's word (the Bible) must remain in us. Our business qualifies for God's power! Our lives qualify for the blessings of God. We are the perfect candidates to receive whatever it is we ask for! But first, commit to remain in Christ.

Now as you follow Jesus Christ, and keep his words close to you, you have the right and the authority to pray to God in JESUS'S NAME, and receive what you ask for. This is how true manifestation of God's power happens in our lives. Now take your request to God and know he hears you and it shall come to pass! Whether it's for business ideas, financial provision to expand your business, or for personal reasons that only you know about! Pray and Seek God in Jesus Name, and it shall be established!

Prayer: Lord, I thank you for sending your Son Jesus Christ. Your word says in John 15:7 that as I remain in Christ, I may ask whatever I wish in his name and it will be done for me. I come to you now in the area of my business (insert you own personal request here!) in Jesus Name. I declare that I will see business success this year. I pray that you supernaturally catapult me so that my business reaches great success that doesn't take years to accomplish in Jesus Name. I pray that you are attentive to my prayers and that you are with me providing guidance along the way. In Jesus Name.

Write to God

Take this time to write all of your request out to God. In Jesus Name. Have faith that it is already done!

_____

_____

_____

_____

_____

_____

_____

_____

_____

_____

_____

_____

_____

_____

_____

_____

Day 12: Faith + Works

"Just as the body is dead without breath, so also faith is dead without good works" James 2: 26

"Don't you remember that our ancestor Abraham was shown to be right by God by his actions when he offered his son Isaac on the altar? You see, his faith and his actions worked together. His actions made his faith complete". James 2: 21-22

Faith is more than a mental thought of belief. Your mouth can say that you believe, and your actions can show God the complete opposite. God says that if you say you believe, but your actions say otherwise, your faith is actually dead. It does not exist. Like Abraham, our faith is complete when our actions back it up. When we show God that we truly believe him through our actions, we activate his superpower.

This applies especially to your business. Imagine you pray, "Lord bless me with 1 million dollars in my business. Help me be successful", but then you simply sit down on your couch and watch to see if your bank account changes. You're hoping for a change in a number, but you are not actually doing the work for God to bless. You see, the proper response to that prayer would be to get to work with great expectation that God is going to bless the work that you do.

As you work on your business, you must know in your heart and mind that whatever you produce, God is going to bless it. You prayed a prayer of faith, and your actions are completing that prayer. Your actions of working are proving to God that you actually have faith that he can bless you.

Another mistake you can make after saying that prayer is working non-stop all day everyday hoping that the work you are doing will equal to 1 million dollars. That in itself is doubtful to God. True faith in this situation is you believing that no matter the amount of work you put in (big or small), God can bless it and make it worth millions. Not because of the amount of work you are putting in, but because you prayed in faith, and you believe that the work you are doing is capable of being blessed by God.

Prayer: Lord, I thank you for blessing me. I thank you God that I can come to you in faith, and make my request known to you. There is no request too big or too small for you to handle. I thank you that I don't have to work day in and day out to receive your blessings. I thank you that you love me. Lord I pray that as I build my business and grow it to the next level, that you are blessing me tremendously. I thank you now Lord for the supernatural things you are going to do in and through my business. In Jesus Name, Amen.

Write to God

Declare your faith in God today. Write to him. Write out your business thoughts. Where are you in your business? What doubts are you having? Write out your prayers to God regarding these matters. Write out the actions you will take today.

_____

_____

_____

_____

_____

_____

_____

_____

_____

_____

_____

_____

Day 13: Wealth Comes Easy

You may say in your heart, 'My power and the strength of my hand made me this wealth'. But you shall remember the LORD, your God, for it is He who is giving you power to make wealth, that He may confirm His covenant which He swore to your fathers, as it is this day. Deuteronomy 8:17-18 NASB

What a powerful and comforting scripture to read as we build and grow our businesses. There is a common misconception in entrepreneurship that in order to "make it" you have to grind. By definition, grind means hard and dull work.

Many people equate entrepreneurship to a constant grind; constantly grinding and putting in hard work in order to reach success. But God tells us that it's not our hands that bring us wealth. It is not our strength or our grind that brings us success. We have the power to produce wealth because of the power God has given to us.

It's comforting to know that I don't have to over exert myself to reach success. God is in control. The power is given from God. God is all mighty. He has all power in his hands. ALL power. We don't have to work ourselves dry, we have God. He has the ability to give us supernatural strength.

The other reassuring side of this is that God is concerned with our wealth. Wealth was a promise given to us through the covenant made with Abraham. Don't think God isn't working on your behalf. He cares about you. You don't have to experience lack because of who you are in God. So today pray for strength, pray for God- given power. Pray for God- ordained wealth.

Prayer: Lord thank you! I thank you because of who you are. I thank you that I don't have to experience lack. Thank you for choosing me. Thank you for loving me. I pray now that you give me the supernatural power to create success and wealth in my business. I know it's not because of what I do, but it's because of who you are. You are all powerful. You are all mighty. Because you are a promise keeper, I don't have to be without. I never have to experience lack ever again. For that Lord I say thank you. In Jesus Name, Amen.

Write to God

Do you feel like you have to constantly grind? How can you change your habits from "grinding" or working from sun up to sun down to healthy habits of trusting God?

_____

_____

_____

_____

_____

_____

_____

_____

_____

_____

_____

_____

_____

_____

_____

Day 14: No Worries

"For this reason, I say to you, do not be worried about your life, as to what you will eat or what you drink; nor for your body as to what you will put on. Is not life more than food, and the body more than clothing? Look at the birds of the air, that they do not sow, nor reap, not gather into barns, yet your heavenly Father feeds them. Are you not worth much more than they? And who of you by being worried can add a single hour to his life?" Matthew 6: 25-27 NASB.

In business, you may be tempted to worry about your financial situation. You may even allow your current financial situation to determine how hard you work in your business. But I urge you to remember that it is not by your own power or your own strength that you are able to add more wealth to your life. God is the one who has given us the power to create wealth.

Now you may say, but I am in need. I need to make more money for this, and that, and that may be true. You may need more resources for your current apparent needs. I've been in situations of need; where rent needs to be paid in a few weeks or I am needing to purchase something for my business. And in those instances, I remember Matthew 6. God promises me that there is no need to worry.

As humans, worry is a trait that we often have. But as children of God, we have the power to push it away. No matter how scary a situation may look, God has us covered. God loves you. He will not allow you to lack as you stay in him. He says look at the birds, they don't even understand the basic biblical principles of sowing and reaping, and yet I still provide for them. He then goes to ask, are you not worth more than a bird? Well, what do you think? Are you? You are.

You are a child of God. Think of an earthly parent and child. Most parents understand their children's needs and will go to lengths to make sure they have whatever that is. God goes far beyond that. Verse 32 and 33 goes on to say "For your heavenly Father knows that you need all of these things. But seek first His Kingdom, and all these things will be added to you."

As we continue to seek God during this process, every need that we have will be covered and taken care of. Believe that.

Prayer: Thank you God for not forgetting me. Thank you for being a gracious and loving father. I thank you that you are providing for all of my needs. I have no worry. I have no doubt. I have faith that you are capable to take care of me. I thank you that in you I have everything I could ever want and need. You are all I need. As I continue to seek you and your Kingdom, I pray you continually add to my life every need that I have. In Jesus Name, Amen.

Write to God

All of your needs are being met now. Everything that you are looking for, God is providing it now. Today just write to God and thank Him. Thank Him for everything that you are believing him for. If you are believing him for financial provision, thank Him for the financial breakthrough he is bringing to your life right now. Remember we must walk in faith with God. He moves to our faith in him.

Day 15: Who Do You Work For?

Commit your works to the Lord [submit and trust them to Him], and your plans will succeed [if you respond to His will and guidance] Proverbs 16:3 AMP

As you are planning out your business ideas and strategies, I encourage you to include God along every step. Submit your plans to him. Trust God with them. Now what does this look like? As you are sitting down preparing for business, have meetings with God. Talk to him. Ask him what ideas does he have for your business? Ask him to give you supernatural wisdom to implement into your business.

In my business meetings with God, I turn on my worship playlist which is filled with instrumental songs (songs with no words). I allow these to play as I pray to God for business ideas. As I journal out my own plans, I will begin to get ideas from God. You'll know if you are getting ideas from God, because it will be ideas that you've never thought of before. I call these ideas from Heaven.

You can also pray to God for wisdom using James 1:5. God gives wisdom freely to those who ask. But you have to ask. You will begin to think of specific strategies to implement with the ideas from Heaven. This is you submitting your plans to God. To submit means to yield to the authority or will of someone else. Just imagine, you could have ideas directly from God himself. Proverbs

16:3 says your plans WILL succeed if you respect God's will and guidance. Submit your ideas to God today and allow your business to prosper.

Prayer: Father I submit my business to you today. I give every plan and idea to you now. I allow your Holy Spirit to bless my mind with ideas from Heaven. Give me supernatural ideas and strategies to take my business to the next level. My mind is clear now, and I am open to receive what you have for me God. Speak words into my heart now that you want me to take into my business. I trust you with my business. I thank you for blessing me now with ideas and wisdom. In Jesus Name, Amen.

Write to God

Begin to write out your business ideas and allow God to bless you with ideas of his own as you write.

_____

_____

_____

_____

_____

_____

_____

_____

_____

_____

_____

_____

_____

_____

_____

Day 16: Take a Risk!

Farmers who wait for perfect weather never plant. If they watch every cloud, they never harvest. Just as you cannot understand the path of the wind or the mystery of a tiny baby growing in its mother's womb, so you cannot understand the activity of God, who does all things. Plant your seed in the morning and keep busy all afternoon, for you don't know if profit will come from one activity or another-or maybe both. Ecclesiastes 11: 4-6 NLT

Starting and running a business comes with a lot of risks. Naturally, you'll want to make the decision that is most sure to work; the decision that will bring you the largest return on your investment. Because of this, many people get stuck waiting on the right opportunity. They wait, hoping for the perfect time to come along before they move on a business idea. Even the Bible says that he who waits will never plant. You're waiting on the perfect opportunity to come, but God says go. Be wise in your decisions, pray for peace, and GO!

If you never plant, then you can never reap a harvest. If you never put the work in, there is no way you can have success. You reap what you sow, is not a cliché saying, its scripture. God works off of sowing and reaping. Galatians 6:7 reads, "Do not be deceived, God is not mocked; for whatever a man sows, this and this only is what he reaps."

The ways of God are mysterious. He will not share every detail with you, because then you will have no need for faith. As God blesses you with business ideas, go and put them into action. God requires faith. He requires movement. He blesses your obedience and your faith, not your carefulness and fear.

What's holding you back on your next business decision?

I love the instructions and hope given in verse 6. Solomon tells us to plant our seed in the morning and keep busy. Put in the necessary work as soon as you can, and as you do that, don't watch over the seed. Don't keep checking back to see if what you did actually worked. Put another idea in motion. Plant your seeds and keep working. You never know which idea will produce a harvest. It can be idea 1, it can be idea 5, it can be every idea. But you won't know until you get to work. God won't bless what doesn't exist. And God will not bless your doubt. Plant your seed; produce your 1st idea, and keep it going! Believe in faith that God will bless your work, and in the meantime, continuing producing seeds that could one day also be blessed.

Prayer: God bless me with supernatural business ideas today. Help me to plant each seed in faith. As I plant my business seeds this week, I pray that you come and bless what I sow so that it produces a harvest. Lord I trust you. My complete faith is in you. I will not look back. I pray that as I finish planting one seed, you give me another seed to plant. I pray that you give me continual business ideas to implement into my business. In Jesus Name, I pray that you bless every seed that I plant. For I know your word says, that without sowing, there is no reaping. So, God, please bless my seed and allow your principles to apply to my business today. Allow every seed to reap a harvest. In Jesus Name, Amen.

Write to God

You prayed a prayer of faith, now write down every business idea that you can commit to putting in motion this week! Write down the ideas and start making it happen this week. As you move on throughout the devotions this week, continually come back to today, Day 16, and cross off each idea that you've successfully sown.

_____

_____

_____

_____

_____

_____

_____

_____

_____

_____

_____

_____

_____

Section 3: Running the Business

Every scripture, devotional, and prayer listed above can and should be used even while running your business. But, in this section we will go more in depth with how God wants you to run your business as it relates to faith, dealing with your money, connecting with different people, and more.

You've built the foundation in Christ, now it's time to run your business and become even more successful.

Day 17: More than You Can Imagine!

Now to Him who is able to [carry out His purpose and] do superabundantly more than all that we dare ask or think [infinitely beyond our greatest prayer, hopes, or dreams] according to His power that is at work within us Ephesians 3:20 AMP

As you begin to run your business, know now that God is able to do more than you can ask or even think of. Don't limit God as you are running your business. Don't think that a certain idea will produce $5,000, while another idea may produce $2,000, so because of that, you must produce ideas 3 and 4 to make a total of $20,000. That is a very limiting statement. You have no idea what God is capable of. He can meet your basic needs of producing $20,000 from ideas 1-4, or he could move on his own behalf and allow ideas 1 and 2 to bring you 1 million dollars.

You don't know how God wishes to move in your life and at what capacity. So do the work, have faith, and allow God to do the rest. Believe that God is supplying your needs. Believe God is working in you and your business to serve a greater purpose. And greater purpose oftentimes calls for a greater need. Trust God. He can do more than you can ask or think. He can do more than you hope and pray for. Simply pray for God's hand over your business. His power is at work in us to get done what he wants done in our lives.

Prayer: Lord, I want to live an Ephesians 3:20 lifestyle. I give you complete control to do MORE in me. Do more than I can ask or think. Do more than I can hope or pray for. I give you room Holy Spirit to work in me. Produce fruit in my life. Produce fruit in my business. I will stay out of your way. I will no longer limit you. You are all mighty and all powerful. I love you. Thank you. In Jesus name, Amen.

Write to God

Write thanks to God today for what he has already done in your life, and for what he will do soon through you and your business.

_____

_____

_____

_____

_____

_____

_____

_____

_____

_____

_____

_____

_____

_____

Day 18: Watch Your Connections

Do not be yoked together with unbelievers. For what do righteousness and wickedness have in common? Or what fellowship can light have with darkness? What harmony is there between Christ and Belial. Or what does a believer have in common with an unbeliever?... Therefore "Come out from them and be separate, says the Lord. Touch no unclean thing and I will receive you." 2 Corinthians 6: 14-18

Watch who you allow yourself to connect to. Yes, even in business or should I say especially in business, rightful connections matter. The Bible reads in 1 Corinthians 15:33, Bad moral corrupts good character. You may be someone who's honest, and trustworthy but your connections will speak for you. As you are expanding and looking to grow supernaturally in your business, don't allow for connections that look good on paper to fool you or wipe you off of your feet.

You must have discernment to know who to work with and who not to work with. This could come in the way of big corporations looking to sponsor your business, or a possible mentor who wants to aid you in the growth process. Yes, you will want help from wise counsel along the way, but it's important to pay attention to who that counsel is.

Pray for wisdom and discernment when it comes to partnering with people within your business. If you're needing assistance in any area of your business, pray that God brings the right people into your life who can help elevate you while also being good company.

Prayer: Lord I cancel any business connection that is not sent from you. I pray that you give me discernment in this season, so I know who to connect with and who to avoid as you continue to expand my business. I trust your convictions. I pray that you bring rightful connections that will help me go to the next level in my business. In Jesus Name, Amen.

Write to God

Write down some non-negotiable traits for people you decide to connect with in business. What characteristics must they have? What characteristics must they not have? As you write these down, assess who is currently around you? Do they make the cut?

_____

_____

_____

_____

_____

_____

_____

_____

_____

_____

_____

_____

_____

_____

Day 19: Keep Your Eyes on Him

Again, the devil took him to a very high mountain and showed him all the kingdoms of the world, and their splendor. "All this I will give you," he said, "if you will bow down and worship me." Jesus said to him, "Away from me, Satan! For it is written: 'Worship the Lord your God and serve him only.' Then the devil left him, and the angels came and attended him Matthew 4: 8-11 NIV

If Jesus himself was tempted, we are not above temptation. Jesus had just completed a fast for 40 days and 40 nights, and he was hungry, as shown in verse 2 of this same passage. It was at the time when he was done fasting, and he was getting hungry, that the enemy appeared to him to tempt him with the very thing he was hungry for. He first tempted him with food. He then tempted him to throw himself off of the mountains, and lastly, he tempted him with power and fame. Satan had the authority to tempt Jesus!

As you are consecrating yourself right now in God's word through this devotional, you too are becoming hungry. You may be getting hungry for God's power in your life. You may be becoming hungry for great success in your business. No matter what it is you are hungry for, know that there will be temptation. This is not a statement to be afraid of, rather a statement to prepare you. You see, throughout this devotional you've learned the promises God has for you. You've learned how God wants to bless you. You've learned all of this in preparation. You can now confidently say no to all temptations. You don't need anything that is offered by the enemy.

You don't have to lie to reach success. You don't have to cheat people to rise higher in power and fame. You don't have to connect with wicked people to become more recognized. Any idea or opportunity that "randomly" pops up to suggest any of the former is just a temptation from the tempter himself. Instead of considering the benefits of doing things the world's way, you are now prepared to stand your ground and say "NO!". You don't have to do things the way everyone else is doing them, you don't have to go against your moral understanding to gain power and fame.

James 1:13-17 reads, when tempted, no one should say "God is tempting me." For God cannot be tempted by evil, nor does he tempt anyone; but each person is tempted when they are dragged away by their own evil desire and enticed. Then, after desire has conceived, it gives birth to sin; and sin, when it is full grown, gives birth to death. Don't be deceived, my brothers and sisters. Every good and perfect gift is from above, coming down from the Father of the heavenly lights, who does not change like shifting shadows.

God does not tempt, and he will not put evil in your face. Whenever temptations come, like Jesus, you have the authority to cast the thought and temptation away. God has good and perfect things for your business and your life. The perfect and good things of God will never come from evil.

Prayer: I thank you God that you will never tempt me to go against what is right. I thank you for giving me the same power and authority you gave your son, Jesus Christ. With that power I have the right to tell temptation no, and it must flee immediately. I thank you God that your power is great! I thank you that you have good and perfect things coming to my business now. I trust you and love you. In Jesus Name.

Write to God

What have you been tempted with lately? Write those things down!
Now combat the temptation by doing things God's way!

_____

_____

_____

_____

_____

_____

_____

_____

_____

_____

_____

_____

_____

_____

_____

_____

_____

Day 20: Power and Authority

"But you belong to God, my dear children. You have already won a victory over those people, because the Spirit who lives in you is greater than the spirit who lives in the world" 1 John 4:4 NLT

Do you know you were bought at a special price? Jesus Christ came to this earth and died for your and my sins. What a precious gift. After Jesus died and then rose again, he ascended into heaven. As Jesus rose into heaven, his Spirit descended. Now we have the honor to live on this earth with God's Spirit here to keep us and save us.

One of the best things about having access to the Holy Spirit is that it offers us supernatural authority and power while on earth. Essentially the same power Jesus had while he was here, we now have through his Spirit. You have that power in your business. You have that power in your home and with your family. You have that power in every area of your life.

That authority allows you the right to cancel every attack of the enemy. It's important to understand the power you have as you grow in Christ, and in your business. Whenever you feel as though things are not going right, and you know it's not of God, recite this scripture over your life. "Greater is he who is in me, than he who is in the world!" (King James Version). Whenever you feel as though something isn't going right in your day, or in life, at ANY TIME, declare this scripture out loud and demand your life to line up with this scripture.

Sickness does not have the power to come over your body. Death cannot come in your family before its time. Confusion cannot come in your business ever. Because greater is HE who is in you, than he who is in the earth. God's power is greater than the enemy's power. No weapon of hell can affect your life ever. The devil's devices do not have any power over you. Ever! In Jesus Name. Declare that declaration over your home, your life, your family, and your business, often! You have power.

Prayer: Lord I thank you for your divine power. I thank you that you, who lives in me, are far more powerful than the enemy. Thank you for your hedge of protection surrounding my home, and my family now in Jesus Name. I declare the blood of Jesus now to protect me in every area of my life. Thank you for sending your Son to die for my sins, so now I may live and live life more abundantly. Thank you for your mercy. I declare and decree every power of hell must go from my life now. I declare that Satan has NO power over my life. Every plan from hell must be canceled now in Jesus Name. I thank you God that you have not given me a spirit of Fear, but of a sound mind. I thank you God that your word says that your perfect love cancels out all fear. Because of your perfect love for me, I have nothing to be afraid of. I pray that you cover me now with your protective wings as said in Psalm 91. Thank you, God, for what you have already done. In Jesus Name, Amen!

Write to God

How can you utilize God's power and authority in your life today?

_____

_____

_____

_____

_____

_____

_____

_____

_____

_____

_____

_____

_____

_____

_____

_____

Day 21: The Peace of God

Do not be anxious about anything, but in every situation, by prayer and petition, with thanksgiving, present your request to God. And the peace of God, which transcends all understanding, will guard your hearts and minds in Christ Jesus Philippians 4:6-7 NIV

Peace is a perfect gift given from God. Jesus Christ is known as the prince of peace. (Isaiah 9:6) Jesus came so that we can have perfect peace while here on this earth. Any emotion that you feel that is the opposite of peace, is not from God.

Now in running a business, you may at times feel frustrated, overwhelmed, worn out, tired, etc, but have peace in knowing that God has given you perfect peace. Whenever you feel emotions opposite of peace, open your mouth and tell them to go, and then follow the instructions given to you in Philippians 4:6-7

Again, it reads, don't be anxious, but with prayer and petition (a formal request or plea), and with thanksgiving (be thankful!) present your request to God. Whatever you are going through, lift it up to God. Pray to him, offer thanksgiving, and then have peace that the situation is taken care of.

We must always give thanks when praying to God. He has already done so much for us. Even when we are in the middle of difficult emotions, there is a reason to thank God. Speaking thanks during prayer is a sign of faith. You're thanking God for what he has already done and what he is getting ready to do. When you pray for something, say thank you as if it's already done.

I love John 16: 33 AMP. It reads, "I have told you these things, so that in Me you may have [perfect] peace. In the world you have tribulation and distress and suffering, but be courageous [be confident, be undaunted, be filled with joy]; I have overcome the world." [My conquest is accomplished, My victory abiding.]

Wow, what a powerful statement! Jesus has already come; he has already accomplished his mission! In that we should have victory alone. Today, choose to have peace. Whatever is holding you back or causing your emotions to be fickle, lay it down; give it to God allow his perfect peace to cover your heart and mind (Philippians 4:7)

Prayer: Lord, I thank you for gifting me with perfect peace. I come to you now in every area of my life that I am struggling. I rebuke all anxious thoughts. I lift my cares to you now in Jesus Name. I thank you that in you I do not have to worry. Every promise of God is yes and amen. In Jesus Name, Amen.

Write to God

Write down every emotion that you have been feeling that does not line up with God's peace; any emotion that contradicts God's word (worry, doubt, anxiety, depression, sadness, etc) Write it down and give it to God. As you write it down, imagine he is taking it and ripping it up. Allow God's peace to change your heart and mind right now.

_____

_____

_____

_____

_____

_____

_____

_____

_____

_____

_____

_____

Day 22: Watch Your Words

"Death and Life are in the power of the tongue, and those who love it and indulge it will eat its fruit and bear the consequences of their words" Proverbs 18:21 AMP

Do you know the power your words have? While running your successful business you must speak words over yourself and your business that represent LIFE and not death. Not even jokingly should you say things that are negative. You could "jokingly" curse yourself without being aware.

Isaiah 55 explains how valuable words are. God says he sends his word out and it accomplishes everything that he assigns it to. We are not God, but we are spiritually made in his image. Just how God is a creator, so are we. Just how God could destroy, so can we. Our words have more power than you could probably ever imagine. You have the ability to say, "My business will be successful this week" and it can happen. You also have the ability to say, "I never get sales", and you won't. Proverbs 18:21 says we will bear the consequences of our words. That can be good consequences or bad.

For the next 7 days, put this into practice. Practice saying positive things over your business, speak things that aren't as if they were! Speak faith declarations over your business. Cancel out any negative thoughts and speaking. Don't allow for yourself or anyone else to speak negative about your business. Monitor your progress as you exercise this. From this moment forward, watch your words. Watch what you say, and how you say it. Understand that whatever you say, it has the capacity to happen.

Prayer: Lord, please forgive me for anything negative I've spoken against myself or anyone else I know; whether it was on purpose or on accident. I break any word curse that I may have said against myself and my business. I declare blessings over my business now in Jesus Name. Help me be more careful with my words from this point forward. In Jesus Name, Amen

Write to God

Write blessings over your business. Whatever you write down, practice saying it over your business every day for at least 1 week.

_____

_____

_____

_____

_____

_____

_____

_____

_____

_____

_____

_____

_____

_____

_____

Day 23: With Faith, Your Words can Literally Move Mountains!

"You don't have enough faith," Jesus told them. "I tell you the truth, if you had faith even as small as a mustard seed, you could say to this mountain, 'Move from here to here,' and it would move. Nothing would be impossible." Matthew 17:20

Declaring "unimaginable" things out loud may seem crazy to some. Could you imagine telling a mountain to move? Would you expect it to actually move when you told it to? The thought of this would make some people laugh out loud.

But Jesus says in Matthew 17:20 that if we had faith as small as a mustard seed it would happen. A mustard seed is one-third the size of an ant. Yes! It's that small. But you have to understand what faith actually means to make sense of this statement. The word faith means to have complete trust or confidence in someone or something. Complete Trust! So, even if you have a small amount of complete trust, that's enough trust to make a mountain move.

The problem with some of us is not that we don't have enough faith; we don't have faith at all. To put complete trust in something, or to believe that without a shadow of a doubt something will happen tends to be like a foreign language to some.

Once, when I was in college, I really put the word faith to use. I didn't have any experience with it, but I knew that faith meant that I couldn't doubt at all. I was set to fail all of my classes, and there was nothing I could do to pass. Everything was completely out of my control being that it was the end of the semester. So, being desperate, I decided to try out faith. I got in the shower and started praying for a miracle. I then made myself declare out loud, "I will pass all of my classes. In Jesus Name, I will pass!". Now at first, I didn't believe this statement when I said it, but I knew that faith meant to believe 100%. So, I stayed in the shower until I believed that declaration. One hour later I got out of the shower, with just an ounce of faith. I believed that I would pass! I also wouldn't allow myself to think about it at all because I was afraid that If I gave it too much thought, I would doubt God's ability. As soon as I got out of the shower, my email notifications started to go off, and each of my professors were sending out mass emails about an overall grade curve being applied to either the final exam or the final course grade. In the end, I passed my classes. My faith the size of a mustard seed worked!

I believe that's the type of faith Jesus is talking about in Matthew 17:20. I have additional faith stories that I will share another day on my YouTube channel: www.youtube.com/natalehnicole. Now I'm not saying use faith as an excuse to not do the work. After that instance in college, I made sure to get all A's in my classes. But in the semester mentioned above, I didn't do the work! I asked God to forgive me, and then I put faith to work. And, it worked! How can you apply real faith in your life today? What about in your business?

Prayer: Lord, I thank you for being an on-time God. I thank you Lord for always being there for me in time of need. I put my complete confidence and trust in you. I know that you have the power to do any and everything. I declare I have faith in your Word. I have faith that you will move in my business. I have faith that I will have a successful business. I have faith in every area of my life. I rebuke all doubt and cancel it now in the name of Jesus. In Jesus Name I pray, Amen.

Write to God

How will you show faith today and this week in your business?

_____

_____

_____

_____

_____

_____

_____

_____

_____

_____

_____

_____

_____

_____

_____

_____

Day 24: Wait! Before You Give Up...

Consider it pure joy, my brothers and sisters, whenever you face trials of many kinds, because you know that the testing of your faith produces perseverance. Let perseverance finish its work so that you may be mature and complete, not lacking anything. James 1:2-4

Blessed is the one who perseveres under trials because, having stood the test, that person will receive the crown of life that the Lord has promised to those who love him. James 1:12

God never promised us that living the faith- filled life would be easy. He makes it clear that we will face trials that will in fact test our faith. Has your faith been tested lately? Can you say that you've passed the test?

Test will arise while running your business. It may even seem like you are being tested every single day, as you are in the growing phase. But remember, the beauty in the test of faith is that when you push past the test, you will experience true perseverance in your business. Yes, you will be stretched; most times past your comfort zone. But, every test of faith in your business that is passed will not only make your business stronger, but you as well.

Faith is an exciting principle to practice in business because in it all you have to do is believe, which I know can be easier said than done. But just imagine, you are having a tough time in business, you don't see how you are able to complete a task at the level that you desire, so you do your best and pray to God to make a miracle happen in that area. Can't you just sense the peace that comes from that? You take all of the pressure off of yourself, and you give it to God.

I can tell you, when applied, faith is a beautiful thing. As a business owner, I exercise faith daily in my business. I receive great ideas almost every day. Like mentioned in Ecclesiastes 11:6 I'm not sure which idea will produce a profit, so I typically try them all. When trying out an idea, I have faith that it'll work, I put in the necessary work, and I allow for God to do the rest. Every time I deposit faith into my business, I receive a harvest from it. What are you depositing into your business today? Is it faith? Hope? Fear? Doubt? Whatever you sow, you will reap.

I experienced a dry season in my business last year just months after starting. When I look back at that time, I was not depositing anything into my business. No faith, no work, no time, nothing. And from that, I reaped absolutely nothing. One day I finally decided to stop pouting, and sow time, faith, and work into my business. What did I reap from that? Sales, new customers, new ideas, and a new drive to continue working! Every day is a new day! Start fresh every morning and deposit faith into your business. No matter what trial you may be facing that day, overcome it with faith. Push past the doubt, and fear & persevere in your business. You will reap a reward from it.

Prayer: Lord, I will not give up in my business today. I thank you that as trials come, I can apply faith to push past them. Thank you for giving me the strength to withstand any obstacles that may come my way. I pray that you have your hand over my business so that I can continue to become successful. I trust you. In Jesus Name, Amen.

Write to God

What trials are you currently facing? Write out a specific game plan for how you plan to use faith and perseverance to push past your current trials.

_____

_____

_____

_____

_____

_____

_____

_____

_____

_____

_____

_____

_____

_____

Day 25: Faithful with Little

"The master said, 'well done, my good and faithful servant. You have been faithful in handling this small amount, so now I will give you many more responsibilities. Let's celebrate together'. To those who use well with what they are given, even more will be given, and they will have an abundance. But those who do nothing, even what little they have will be taken away." Matthew 25:23, 29

What will you do with the little you currently have? God is looking to see if you will sow it to make more or hoard it in fear of losing it all. In this passage from today, a master gave his three servants different bags of talents (silver). The amount he gave to them was based off of how much he knew they could handle. One servant received 5 bags of silver, and he invested it and earned 5 more. The second servant received 2 bags of silver, he went to work and made 2 more. The third servant only received 1 bag of silver, and he hid it so that he could preserve the 1 bag.

When all 3 servants gave a report on what they did with the money, servants 1 and 2 received the congratulatory message from our text today. The third servant however did not please the master, and his bag of silver was given to the first servant who had a total of 10 bags. The servants who were faithful over their original amounts received even more to govern over. God is looking to see if he can trust you with more. What are you doing with the business ideas he's given you? Have you taken the time to invest so that your business can continue to grow? Have you given your time and service to those in need? Are you just keeping your ideas locked in for a rainy day, or for when you have "more time"?

Can you be trusted with the increase you've been praying for? Saving every idea and every penny you earn is just like servant number 3. It's not benefitting anyone, so why would God give you more? Why would he allow you to keep it locked away? Use it before you lose it, is not just a cliché saying.

Notice how their master was already aware of their ability in the beginning! They received what their master knew they could handle. The master knew that his first servant was capable of making an additional 5 bags of silver, so he received 5 bags in the beginning. He also knew the third servant wasn't able to grow even 1 bag, so that is all he received.

Don't be upset with the amount you have right now. Whether that's the number of followers you have on social media, or the amount of money you have in your bank account. Everything that is given to you is based off of your ability. Will you be a good steward over God's people and his wealth?

Compare your business to this parable. How much does God think you can handle? What will you do with what you are given? Every day you are sending a report to God concerning your faithfulness levels. If you are ready for an increase, it's time to show God you are able to steward it responsibly. Be sure to handle with care what you've already been given!

Prayer: Lord help me be a good steward over the blessings you've already given me. I pray for wisdom to properly handle my finances and in my business. I want to prove to you that I am ready for more. Expand my territory. Make me ready for more. Thank you for what you've already blessed me with. I declare that I will handle it well. In Jesus Name, Amen.

Write to God

What has God already given you? Maybe its money, maybe it's a business idea, maybe it's extra time. How can you commit to be a good steward over these gifts?

_____

_____

_____

_____

_____

_____

_____

_____

_____

_____

_____

_____

_____

_____

Day 26: Success Even in Tough Times

"The Lord God is my strength; He will make my feet like deer's feet, and He will make me walk on my high hills." Habakkuk 3:19

I took some time to really study what deer's feet are like to understand the significance of this text. The article I read was titled "Deer's feet make everything deer do possible!" The article went on to describe the structure of deer feet and how no matter the environment, their feet protect them; especially from any type of fall, although they do not fall often. Their feet are perfect for leaping over obstacles that may appear in the roadway. God is making your feet like deer's feet.

You are leaping over obstacles. It makes everything you attempt, possible. You're protected through every trial. You seldom fall, but when you do, your feet make for the perfect landing. Your feet are taking you to higher places. It belongs to you. Your name is already on it; your feet are now just the driver that will get you there. If you've been waiting on an opportunity, or the perfect time, here's your chance. You're well equipped for success with your deer- like feet.

Prayer: Lord, make my feet like deer feet today. Help me leap over any obstacle that comes my way. Take me to my high place with deer- like feet. I declare that I have the strength to accomplish everything I put my mind to. In Jesus Name, Amen.

Write to God

Where is your high place? Where is God taking you? What can you accomplish in your business now with your deer-like feet?

_____

_____

_____

_____

_____

_____

_____

_____

_____

_____

_____

_____

_____

_____

_____

Day 27: Look Up

"Set your mind on things above, not on things on the earth."
Colossians 3:2 NJKV

The more that God has for you is not always staring you right in your face. There are things God has held up for you. Things that he can't give to you yet. Maybe your faith is too low. Maybe you need to mature in a certain area. But God is a good God. He does not give his children things they cannot handle. There are gifts and levels with your name on it that God is going to give you at an appointed time. So, what do you do in that time of waiting? Pray and look up!

Your present situation can be enough to cause you frustration, anxiety, worry, plus a million other emotions. As an entrepreneur you can easily go through all of these emotions on a normal day. You aren't where you want to be yet, but you can see where you're supposed to be. Look up. Look towards God. Look towards what he promised you.

Realize that right now you're simply in a waiting room. You're waiting to be seen by the doctor (God) to assess if you're ready for your next level. So, while in the waiting room, check yourself out. What can you be doing differently? How can you properly prepare for your next level? If you're next level is more finances, are you budgeting now? Are you tithing? Are you preparing to receive the next level of finances? If your next level is more business opportunities, is your current work schedule organized? Do you have procedures and systems in place for a steady workflow? Do you give time to God each day in your business already?

If God can't trust you with your now, he won't give you your next. Get into preparation while in your waiting room. Don't lose hope. God has not forgotten you. Remember that our time is not God's time. God is not obligated to move when we say move. He's sovereign; not a genie in a bottle. Be happy where you are. God is saving you from yourself. He's allowing you to not self-sabotage your next blessing.

Your waiting area is a place of grace. God is allowing you to be still, look up to him, assess your current situation, and fix yourself before going to your next level and season. Thank God now for not giving you your next level pre-maturely. Wouldn't you rather receive when you're ready, rather than destroy what you received too soon?

Prayer: Thank you God for this waiting room. Thank you for the opportunity to get my current life together before receiving my next from you. I pray that while I'm in this area of waiting that you show me myself. Show me what areas of my life I need to fine- tune. I give my faulty areas to you now. Fix me. Mold me. Prune me. In Jesus Name, Amen.

Write to God

Where is God taking you next? Either he showed you, or you have the desire to go somewhere. Where is that next place? What can you be doing now to prepare for that place?

_____

_____

_____

_____

_____

_____

_____

_____

_____

_____

_____

_____

_____

_____

_____

Day 28: Write the vision, make it plain!

Then the Lord answered me and said: "Write the vision and make it plain on tablets, that he may run who reads it. For the vision is yet for an appointed time; but at the end it will speak, and it will not lie. Though it tarries, wait for it; because it will surely come, it will not tarry." Habakkuk 2:2-3 NKJV

Whatever dream, idea, or plan God gives you, write it down. Don't forget it or lose hope. Don't assume it's not going to happen because you've waited a while. God gives us visions and dreams for a later time. The purpose for them is so that we may accurately prepare for what is up ahead. God loves us and desires to protect us.

The word tarry means to delay or be tardy in the act of doing something. Notice how verse 3 says though it may tarry, wait for it; because in the end it will come, and it will not tarry. How in the same verse can God tell us it will tarry, but it will not tarry? You see, to us, it'll feel like the promises of God are coming slow and are extremely delayed. But God assures us that in the end, it actually came right on time. In the end, there was no tarry at all. In the end, you'll appreciate the "tarrying" that happened on your end; you'll appreciate the perfection of God's timing.

Look over your life. Are there things that you had to wait on and in the end when you finally received it, you understood why you had to wait? A season of waiting is not to torment you; it's to protect you. Your season of waiting is to prepare you. Eyes have not seen, ears have not heard, nor has it entered into the hearts of man, what God has prepared for you! (1 Corinthians 2:9)

Write down the vision God has given you. Make it plain. It will not go to waste. It will not go in vain. It shall be established on the earth, as it is already established in heaven. There are things already established in Heaven on your behalf. God already has what you're dreaming of prepared for you. Get into a stance of expectation. Get into a place of FAITH. Get ready to receive.

Prayer: Thank you Jesus for the vision you've given me. Thank you, God, for showing me now the big plans you have for my life. I thank you that you have a place prepared for me already in Heaven. I thank you that what is prepared in heaven is now being established on this earth. I pray that you open my eyes to see you God. Open my eyes so that I may see where you are taking me next. Direct my path Lord. Lead me where you want me to go. In Jesus Name, Amen.

Write to God

Write the vision down that God has given you. Make it plain!

_____

_____

_____

_____

_____

_____

_____

_____

_____

_____

_____

_____

_____

_____

_____

_____

Day 29: Who are You Working For?

"Whatever you do [whatever your task may be], work from the soul [that is, put in your best effort], as [something done] for the Lord and not for men, knowing [with all certainty] that it is from the Lord [not from men] that you will receive the inheritance which is your [greatest] reward. It is the Lord Christ whom you [actually] serve." Colossians 3:23-24

One of the most important lessons I've learned while in business is to constantly remember who I am in business for, and why I am in business. No matter what your personal, intrinsic motivation is for starting a business, remember that you are in business for God and not for yourself. God gave you the desire to start a business, and it is going to be used for a purpose way bigger than you, if you allow it. This is how you get the most fulfilment out of your work. This is how you persevere when it gets difficult. This is how you remain open to receive whatever it is God wants to do in and through you.

I started my business thinking I would just be selling clothes. When things did not go the way that I expected in the beginning, I started to custom create faith-based apparel. From there I became more open about my faith on my social media platforms. That turned into me speaking more about my faith journey on my YouTube channel. Which then turned into this devotional.

Daily I allow God into my business. Daily I allow for the Holy Spirit to do what he wants with my platform. As I remain open, my business constantly changes. And with each change, comes new profitable ideas.

The best way to progress in business is to remain open while also not working to please man. Yes, your business will be used to help those around you, but most people don't know exactly how they need help. Allow God to move in your business. He will position you so your gifts can be exposed in a way that you didn't even know was possible. God knows what's inside of you. He knows how your personal attributes can be best used to help those in need.

You may have a great idea for how you want to be used through your business, but God knows all. Be used for a greater purpose.

Prayer: God, I allow you to use me today. Use my business for a purpose bigger than me. Expose my gifts in such a way that it positively impacts those around me. I allow you to enter into my business. Do great and mighty things through me and my business. In Jesus Name, Amen.

Write to God

What are you good at? What do you enjoy doing? Write these things down. Now think of how those things can be used in partnership with your business? How can you help those around you by doing those activities? Allow God to use your business in a new way today.

_____

_____

_____

_____

_____

_____

_____

_____

_____

_____

_____

_____

Day 30: Be a Doer!

"Do not merely listen to the word, and so deceive yourselves. Do what it says. Anyone who listens to the word but does not do what it says is like someone who looks at his face in a mirror and, after looking at himself, goes away and immediately forgets what he looks like. But whoever looks intently into the perfect law that gives freedom and continues in it- not forgetting what they have heard but doing it-they will be blessed in what they do." James 1:22-25 NIV

As we finish this devotional, I encourage you to keep every scripture, prayer, and intimate thoughts with God close to your heart. God wants to move in your life; he wants to move in your business. God wants to elevate you to the next level, but each step listed is imperative for that to happen. As you finish this devotional, I want you to keep the momentum going with your faith in God. Remember God's ear is attentive to you when you pray, seek him, and turn from your wicked ways. Continue to pray and seek him daily.

When times get tough, don't forget the word of God. When things aren't going the way you want, remember faith! God is ready and looking for individuals who are open to letting him rule in their lives. He's looking for businesses and platforms that can be used for his glory. Allow your business to be a vessel. Be used for a purpose bigger than you. Be blessed to bless others.

Prayer: God, I thank you for what you have done and are currently doing in my business. Lord, I allow myself to be used by you for a greater purpose. Use my business for your glory. Lead me down the path you want me to take. Open doors that only you can open. Bring supernatural partnerships and opportunities that only you can bring. In Jesus Name, Amen

Write to God

Write a letter to God thanking him for blessing your business and outlining the plans you have for your business and asking him to lead, guide and direct your steps.

_____

_____

_____

_____

_____

_____

_____

_____

_____

_____

_____

_____

_____

_____

Free Space to Journal
Write to God

Date: _____

_____

_____

_____

_____

_____

_____

_____

_____

_____

_____

_____

_____

_____

_____

_____

_____

Write to God

_____

_____

_____

_____

_____

_____

_____

_____

_____

_____

_____

_____

_____

_____

_____

_____

_____

_____

_____

_____

Write to God

Date: _____

Write to God

Date: _____

_____

_____

_____

_____

_____

_____

_____

_____

_____

_____

_____

_____

_____

_____

_____

_____

_____

_____

Write to God

Write to God

Date: _____

_____

_____

_____

_____

_____

_____

_____

_____

_____

_____

_____

_____

_____

_____

_____

_____

_____

_____

_____

_____

Write to God

Date: _____

_____

_____

_____

_____

_____

_____

_____

_____

_____

_____

_____

_____

_____

_____

_____

_____

_____

_____

_____

Write to God

Date: _____

_____

_____

_____

_____

_____

_____

_____

_____

_____

_____

_____

_____

_____

_____

_____

_____

_____

_____

_____

_____

Write to God

Date: _____

_____

_____

_____

_____

_____

_____

_____

_____

_____

_____

_____

_____

_____

_____

_____

_____

_____

_____

_____

_____

Write to God

Date: _____

Write to God

Date: _____

_____

_____

_____

_____

_____

_____

_____

_____

_____

_____

_____

_____

_____

_____

_____

_____

_____

_____

_____

_____

_____

_____

Write to God

_____

_____

_____

_____

_____

_____

_____

_____

_____

_____

_____

_____

_____

_____

_____

_____

_____

_____

_____

_____

Write to God

Date: _____

Write to God

Date: _____

_____
_____
_____
_____
_____
_____
_____
_____
_____
_____
_____
_____
_____
_____
_____
_____
_____
_____
_____
_____
_____

Write to God

Date: _____

_____

_____

_____

_____

_____

_____

_____

_____

_____

_____

_____

_____

_____

_____

_____

_____

_____

_____

_____

Write to God

_____

_____

_____

_____

_____

_____

_____

_____

_____

_____

_____

_____

_____

_____

_____

_____

_____

_____

_____

Write to God

Date: _____

_____

_____

_____

_____

_____

_____

_____

_____

_____

_____

_____

_____

_____

_____

_____

_____

_____

_____

_____

Write to God

_____

_____

_____

_____

_____

_____

_____

_____

_____

_____

_____

_____

_____

_____

_____

_____

_____

_____

_____

_____

Write to God

Date: _____

_____

_____

_____

_____

_____

_____

_____

_____

_____

_____

_____

_____

_____

_____

_____

_____

_____

_____

_____

_____

Write to God

Write to God

Date: _____

_____

_____

_____

_____

_____

_____

_____

_____

_____

_____

_____

_____

_____

_____

_____

_____

_____

_____

Write to God

Date: _____

Write to God

Date: _____

_____

_____

_____

_____

_____

_____

_____

_____

_____

_____

_____

_____

_____

_____

_____

_____

_____

_____

_____

_____

Write to God

Date: _____

Write to God

Date: _____

Write to God

Date: _____

Write to God

Date: _____

_____

_____

_____

_____

_____

_____

_____

_____

_____

_____

_____

_____

_____

_____

_____

_____

_____

_____

_____

_____

_____

Write to God

Date: _____

_____

_____

_____

_____

_____

_____

_____

_____

_____

_____

_____

_____

_____

_____

_____

_____

_____

_____

_____

_____

Write to God

Date: _____

_____

_____

_____

_____

_____

_____

_____

_____

_____

_____

_____

_____

_____

_____

_____

_____

_____

_____

_____

_____

Write to God

Date: _____

Write to God

Date: _____

_____

_____

_____

_____

_____

_____

_____

_____

_____

_____

_____

_____

_____

_____

_____

_____

_____

_____

_____

_____

_____

Write to God

Date: _____

Write to God

Date: _____

Write to God

_____

_____

_____

_____

_____

_____

_____

_____

_____

_____

_____

_____

_____

_____

_____

_____

_____

_____

_____

_____

Write to God

Date: _____

Write to God

_____

_____

_____

_____

_____

_____

_____

_____

_____

_____

_____

_____

_____

_____

_____

_____

_____

_____

_____

_____

Write to God

Date: _____

_____

_____

_____

_____

_____

_____

_____

_____

_____

_____

_____

_____

_____

_____

_____

_____

_____

_____

_____

Write to God

Date: _____

_____

_____

_____

_____

_____

_____

_____

_____

_____

_____

_____

_____

_____

_____

_____

_____

_____

_____

_____

Write to God

Date: _____

_____

_____

_____

_____

_____

_____

_____

_____

_____

_____

_____

_____

_____

_____

_____

_____

_____

_____

_____

_____

_____

Write to God

_____

_____

_____

_____

_____

_____

_____

_____

_____

_____

_____

_____

_____

_____

_____

_____

_____

_____

_____

Write to God

Date: _____

Write to God

_____

_____

_____

_____

_____

_____

_____

_____

_____

_____

_____

_____

_____

_____

_____

_____

_____

_____

_____

Write to God

_____

_____

_____

_____

_____

_____

_____

_____

_____

_____

_____

_____

_____

_____

_____

_____

_____

_____

_____

_____

Write to God

Date: _____

Write to God

_____

_____

_____

_____

_____

_____

_____

_____

_____

_____

_____

_____

_____

_____

_____

_____

_____

_____

_____

_____

Write to God

Date: _____

_____

_____

_____

_____

_____

_____

_____

_____

_____

_____

_____

_____

_____

_____

_____

_____

_____

_____

Write to God

Date: _____

_____

_____

_____

_____

_____

_____

_____

_____

_____

_____

_____

_____

_____

_____

_____

_____

_____

_____

_____

_____

Write to God

Write to God

Date: _____

Write to God

Date: _____

_____

_____

_____

_____

_____

_____

_____

_____

_____

_____

_____

_____

_____

_____

_____

_____

_____

_____

_____

_____

Write to God

Date: _____

_____

_____

_____

_____

_____

_____

_____

_____

_____

_____

_____

_____

_____

_____

_____

_____

_____

_____

_____

_____

Write to God

Date: _____

Write to God

Date: _____

_____

_____

_____

_____

_____

_____

_____

_____

_____

_____

_____

_____

_____

_____

_____

_____

_____

_____

_____

Made in the USA
Columbia, SC
12 May 2020